Jobs in Science

Solve Problems Involving Measurement and Estimation

Holden Strauss

PowerKiDS press™

NEW YORK

Published in 2015 by The Rosen Publishing Group, Inc.
29 East 21st Street, New York, NY 10010

Book Design: Jonathan J. D'Rozario

Photo Credits: Cover Matej Kastelic/Shutterstock.com; pp. 3, 4, 6–24 (background) 123dartist/Shutterstock.com; p. 5 Torsak
Thammachote/Shutterstock.com; p. 7 (main) Tom Grundy/Shutterstock.com; p. 7 (rock insets) photka/Shutterstock.com;
pp. 7, 9 (scale inset) Tihomir Baev/Shutterstock.com; p. 9 (rock insets) vvoe/Shutterstock.com; p. 9 (main) Maridav/
Shutterstock.com; p. 11 Geoffrey Kuchera/Shutterstock.com; p. 13 Dmitry Kalinovsky/Shutterstock.com; p. 15 (main) Adam
Gregor/Shutterstock.com; pp. 15, 17, 21 (beakers) PRILL/Shutterstock.com; p. 17 (main) YanLev/Shutterstock.com; p. 19
Robert Kneschke/Shutterstock.com; p. 21 (main) BMJ/Shutterstock.com; p. 22 Rob Marmion/Shutterstock.com.

Library of Congress Cataloging-in-Publication Data

Strauss, Holden, author.
Jobs in science : solve problems involving measurement and estimation / Holden Strauss.
        pages cm. — (Math masters. Measurement and data)
Includes index.
ISBN 978-1-4777-4912-8 (pbk.)
ISBN 978-1-4777-4913-5 (6-pack)
ISBN 978-1-4777-6461-9 (library binding)
1. Physical measurements—Juvenile literature. 2. Scientists—Juvenile literature. I. Title.
QC39.S843 2015
530.8—dc23

                                    2014007769

Manufactured in the United States of America

CPSIA Compliance Information: Batch #WS15RC: For further information contact Rosen Publishing, New York, New York at 1-800-237-9932.

Contents

What Do Scientists Do?

Do you like to learn about science? There are many kinds of science jobs you can have when you grow up.

Scientists make a lot of measurements. Some scientists have to measure liquids and solids. The amount of matter in a solid object is its mass, which is sometimes called its weight. Scientists use scales to measure mass. The amount of space something takes up in a **container** is its volume. Scientists measure liquid volume using marked containers called beakers.

You can multiply, divide, add, and subtract measurements that have the same units. For example, you can subtract a number measured in grams from another number measured in grams. However, you can't subtract a number measured in kilograms from a number measured in grams.

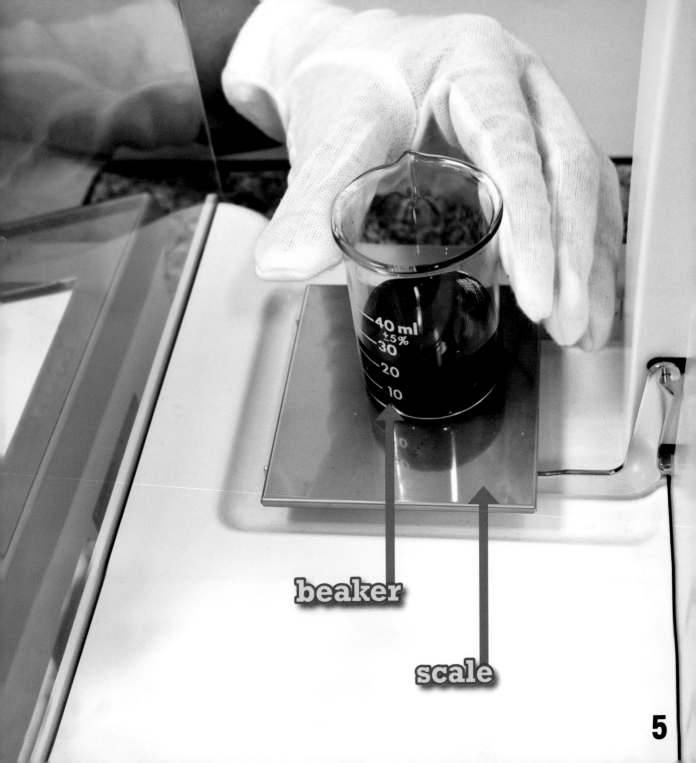

beaker

scale

Measuring Mass

You can think of the amount of matter in something as the amount of "stuff" in it. An object with more matter will usually weigh more than an object with less matter.

Geologists study rocks and minerals. These form the nonliving solid matter that makes up earth. A geologist might weigh a rock to find out more about it. Weight can be measured in grams (g) and kilograms (kg). A geologist uses a scale to find the mass of 2 rocks. The first rock is 1 kilogram, and the second is 5 kilograms.

The scientist holds a third rock in his hand. It feels heavier than the first rock, but lighter than the second rock. Can you estimate the mass? Estimating means guessing based on what you know. You know the third rock weighs between 1 kilogram and 5 kilograms, so you might estimate that it weighs about 3 kilograms.

1 kg

5 kg

mass = ?

Volcanologists are a lot like geologists because they study Earth. They study volcanoes, which are openings in the ground through which melted rock—called lava—sometimes flows. Volcanologists visit volcanoes and collect **samples** of rocks and lava. They can tell when the last **eruption** was, and sometimes they might guess when an eruption will happen again.

Some volcanoes are active, which means they might still erupt. Others are inactive, which means they haven't erupted in a long time. Cooled lava may form a rock called obsidian.

If a volcanologist finds an obsidian rock that's 45 grams and another that's 32 grams, what's their combined mass? To find this answer, add the masses. That makes 77 grams.

 **+**

45 g   32 g

45 grams
+ 32 grams
―――――――
77 grams

Zoologists are scientists who study animals. Some zoologists study animals in the wild. Other zoologists work with animals in zoos. They study how animals look and act, and also how they might have looked and acted throughout history. Some zoologists do experiments with animals. Some come up with ways to keep animal groups alive and well, which is called conservation.

Zoologists sometimes catch wild animals and put special tags on them. This allows zoologists to track animals in the wild. Let's say a zoologist weighs 2 young bobcats he found in the wild.

The bobcats each weigh 10 kilograms. What's their combined mass? Multiply 10 kilograms times 2 to find out. If there's a bobcat kitten that looks half the size of the young bobcats, can you estimate its mass? You could divide 10 kilograms by 2.

10 kilograms x 2 = ? kilograms

10 kilograms ÷ 2 = ? kilograms

Engineers are people who **design** and build machines, products, roads, and many other things. There are different kinds of engineers, but all work with math and science. While they often aren't considered scientists, they use science when working.

Mechanical engineers design and build machines and tools for businesses. Some engineers build computers, while others build machines for factories. Many mechanical engineers today work to make products that save energy. Mechanical engineers build things using different materials, such as plastic, metal, or wood.

An engineer weighs a sheet of metal on a scale and finds that it's 33 kilograms. If the engineer cuts it into 3 equal pieces, how much will each piece weigh? You can divide 33 kilograms by 3 to find your answer.

33 kilograms ÷ 3 = ? kilograms

What's the Volume?

Many scientists work with liquid measurements. Hydrology is the study of water, and hydrologists study water as part of their everyday job. They study what the water is like in an area, how much of it there is, and how easy it is to use.

This job is very important because we use water for almost everything. It's used to make food and to water crops. We also need water to drink. Hydrologists make sure our water is safe. To do this, they take samples of water and test them.

A liter (l) is equal to 1,000 milliliters (ml). A hydrologist gathers 2 samples. You can tell the volume of a sample by looking at the markings on the container. The first sample is 150 milliliters. What's the volume of the water in the second container?

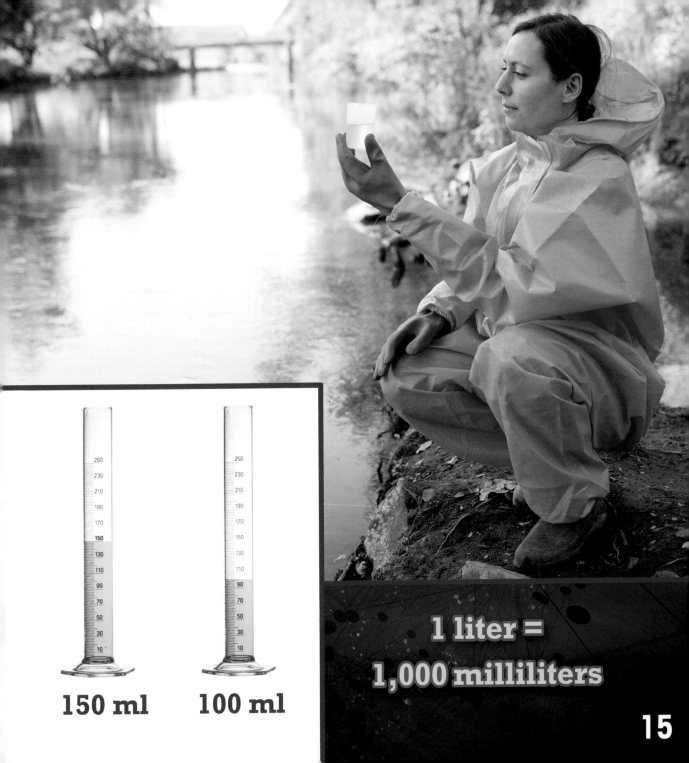

150 ml **100 ml**

1 liter =
1,000 milliliters

Chemists are scientists who study different **chemicals**. They study where to find the chemicals, what they do, how they work, and how they can be used. There are different fields of chemistry. Some chemists study chemicals in plants and animals, while others work to combine chemicals to form something we can use, such as medicine.

Chemists take many measurements when studying how liquid chemicals act. Measurements of chemicals have to be exact in order to get the results the chemist wants.

A chemist has 110 milliliters of a chemical and uses 60 milliliters of it. How much is left?

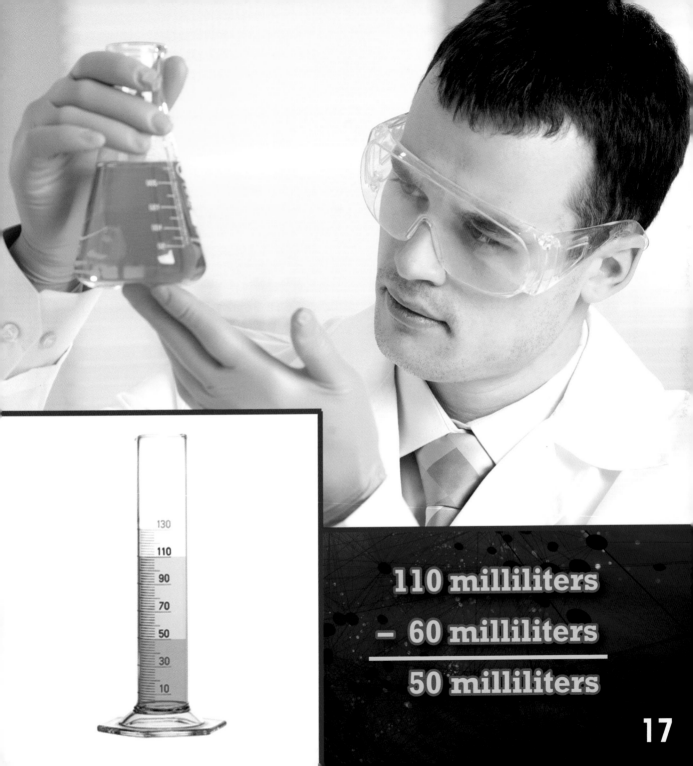

110 milliliters
− 60 milliliters

50 milliliters

17

A pharmacologist (fahr-muh-KAH-luh-jihst) is a lot like a chemist. This scientist works with the chemicals and natural materials used to make medicine.

Pharmacologists study how certain medicines can help or hurt a living thing. Then, they write a report about their findings and sometimes remake the medicine to work better and be safer. This is important because it means the medicine is safe for people to take. Imagine a pharmacologist needs 5 liters of a certain chemical for each batch of medicine.

If the pharmacologist makes 7 batches and uses 5 liters for each batch, how many liters is that altogether?

5 liters x 7 = ? liters

Meteorologists study the weather in our world. They look at maps of clouds and weather systems and **predict** what the weather will be. They also pay attention to temperature, winds, and **precipitation**.

Meteorologists sometimes study the amount of rainfall per year in an area. You can study rainfall, too! Put a rain gauge—a measurement tool for liquids—outside and collect the rainfall. Imagine you measure 150 milliliters of rainfall over the course of 5 days. To find the average rainfall for each day, divide 150 milliliters by 5 days.

There's a big storm on the sixth day. It looks like the storm doubled the amount of rainfall in the rain guage. How can you estimate the amount of rain that fell during the storm?

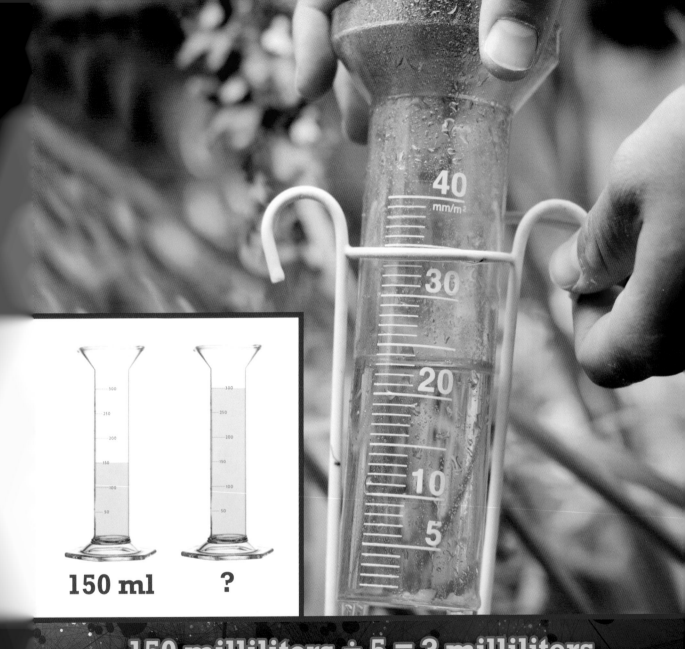

150 ml **?**

150 milliliters ÷ 5 = ? milliliters

150 milliliters x 2 = ? milliliters

You Can Measure, Too

Measuring mass and volume are everyday tasks for many scientists. Scientists can measure the mass of rocks, animals, and plants. They can measure the volume of chemicals, water, and other liquids. This helps them learn about things in our world.

You can measure mass and volume, too! Practice measuring things on scales and comparing the masses of different objects. Practice measuring volume by pouring water into beakers or measuring cups. There are many experiments that you can do at home. You can be a scientist someday!

Glossary

chemical (KEH-mih-kuhl) Matter that can be mixed with other matter to cause changes.

container (kuhn-TAY-nuhr) Something that holds objects or liquids.

design (dih-ZYN) To make a plan for how to make something.

eruption (ih-RUHP-shun) When a volcano gives off lava, ash, and gas.

precipitation (prih-sih-puh-TAY-shun) Water that falls from the sky, including rain, snow, and ice.

predict (prih-DIHKT) To guess what will happen in the future based on facts or knowledge.

sample (SAAM-puhl) An example or bit of something that is used for testing.

Index

Due to the changing nature of Internet links, The Rosen Publishing Group, Inc., has developed an online list of websites related to the subject of this book. This site is updated regularly. Please use this link to access the list: www.powerkidslinks.com/mm/mad/jsci